PLAY WINNING TENNIS

with Perfect Basic Strokes

Book 2

Julio Yacub

Illustrations by Henche Silberstein

Playing Winning Tennis with Perfect Basic Strokes, Book 2

Copyright © 2008 Julio Yacub. All rights reserved. No part of this book may be reproduced or retransmitted in any form or by any means without the written permission of the publisher.

Published by Wheatmark™
610 East Delano Street, Suite 104, Tucson, Arizona 85705 U.S.A.
www.wheatmark.com

ISBN: 978-1-60494-053-4
LCCN: 2008921663

PREFACE

As a self-taught tennis player, I always looked for books that could help me improve my game. Most of the books that I read were long, wordy, and complicated. In college, I had the same problem: books, books, books, but none to my taste, simple but in-depth. I always needed to make outlines to focus on the specific things I wanted to work on. It is true that a good way of learning is to make your own outline, but sometimes we need them ready in order to concentrate on the goals without getting lost in words. This book is written in outline form, and it is simple to follow. You can even take it down to the court and concentrate on any stroke simply by taking a glimpse at that specific page.

Play Winning Tennis with Perfect Basic Strokes is designed for visual learners and students of the game who look for simplicity without cutting corners, but it is not picture-perfect. In this ever-changing game, where there are many stances, several ways to take the racquet back, hit the ball, and follow through, it would be impossible for me to include everything. That's why I laid out this book as a guide, so you can understand how biomechanics work in tennis, and, with the help of your local pro, I hope you can improve your tennis game dramatically.

Even though the drawings and diagrams are shown from a right-handed player's perspective, any left-handed player can interpret them by using a mirror image view. I included side and front views for most of the strokes so the conversion would be easier. Also, to better understand the court diagrams, place yourself in it or imagine that you are on the court playing that particular pattern (instead of just thinking player A and player B). Finally, when using the terms "he" and "his," I imply, by all means, "she" and "hers."

Julio Yacub

ACKNOWLEDGMENT

I must mention that without the help of many people I would not be the person and player that I am today. I would like to thank my mentors, Nick Bollettieri, Vic Braden, and Dennis Van Der Meer, for their continuous contributions to the game and my tennis life.

A special thanks to Jack Groppel and Jim Loehr, who enlightened me to the realms of sport psychology and biomechanics (when they talk...I listen!). I would also like to extend my warmest gratitude to my first coach Ron Steele, former head coach of the Israeli Davis Cup team, for taking me under his wing when I was nothing. Thanks to the USTA High Performance Coaching Program team, especially to Nick Saviano and Paul Lubbers, for raising the stakes in American coaching. Sincere appreciation to my friends John Lapham and Claudio Yamus...and to all my students for sticking with me all these years...you have been the source of my inspiration.

Finally, and most importantly, I would like to thank my family, especially my wife Maura and my mother Henche Silberstein, without whose contributions and support this book would be just a fantasy.

This book belongs to the instructional tennis series "Play Winning Tennis," which covers every aspect of the complete competitive player.

- Book 1: *Playing Winning Tennis with Perfect Fundamentals*
- Book 2: *Playing Winning Tennis with Perfect Basic Strokes*
- Book 3: *Playing Winning Tennis with Perfect Specialty Shots*
- Book 4: *Playing Winning Tennis with Perfect Strategy*
- Book 5: *If I Play Better Tennis, Why Can't I Win?*

LEGEND

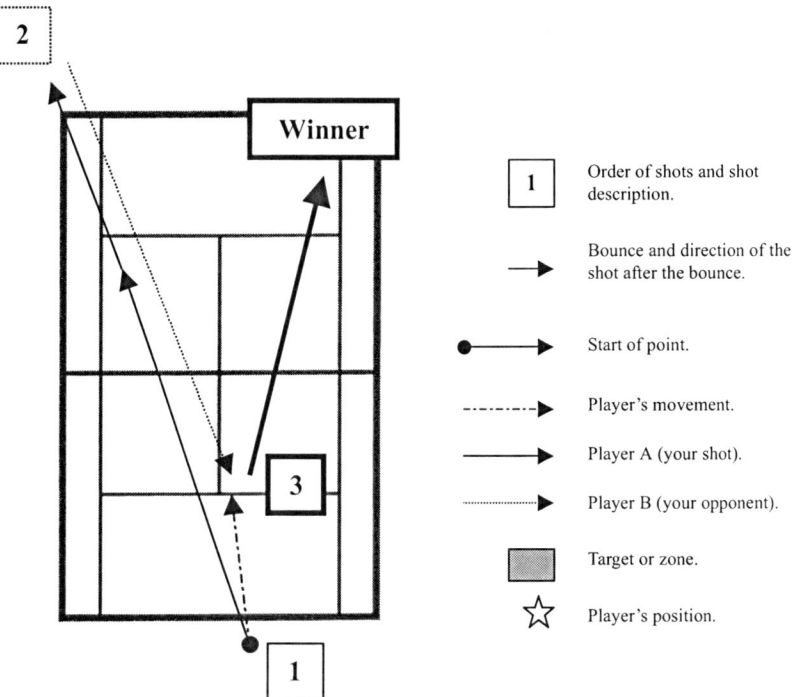

NOTE:
- All diagrams are shown from a right-handed player's perspective, and, unless mentioned, all patterns are identical from the ad or deuce courts, consequently, easily convertible for left-handed players as well as for planning a strategy from both courts. (Patterns are based on geometry of the court and percentage, not player's strength or weakness).
- All "order of shots and shot description" boxes are border coded with the respective shot (line) for easy recognition.

BOOK 2: PLAY WINNING TENNIS
WITH PERFECT BASIC STROKES

FOREHAND 7

BACKHAND 25

VOLLEY 51

SERVE 73

RETURN OF SERVE 87

OVERHEAD 105

FOREHAND

WITH PERFECT BASIC STROKES

FOREHAND

The Big Weapon

By nature, the forehand is a very powerful shot because most of the palm of the dominant hand is behind the grip. Since the forehand is the most frequently used stroke in a rally, it is commonly developed into a weapon to control the point and to win points.

Also, an aggressive attacker should use the forehand to open up the court or to set up a volley. Players like Jim Courier use the forehand for most shots by running around the backhand, hitting an inside-out crosscourt forehand, and forcing the opponent to hit a low percentage down the line.

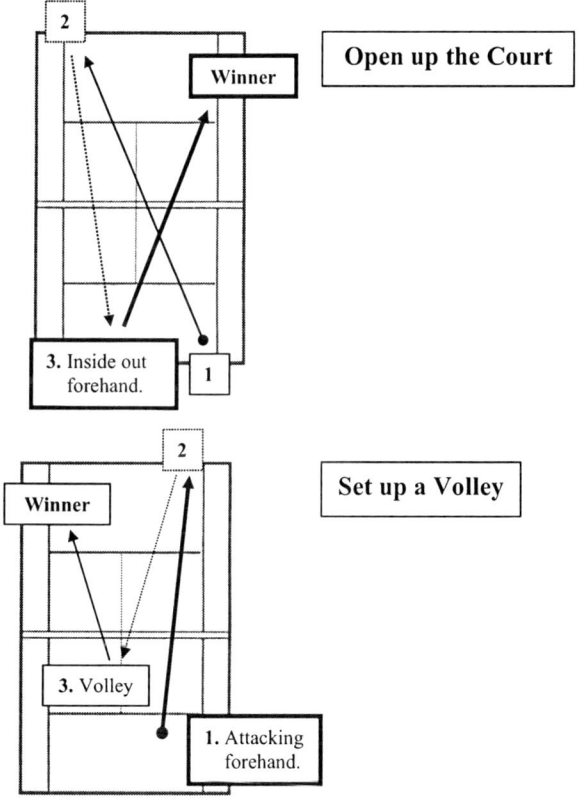

PLAY WINNING TENNIS

TOPSPIN FOREHAND *FRONT VIEW*

1. Split Step / React   2. Footwork

3. Early Preparation   4. Stop and Step

5. Point of Contact   6. Follow Through   7. Recovery

TOPSPIN FOREHAND *SIDE VIEW*

1. Split Step / React   2. Footwork   3. Early Preparation

4. Stop and Step

5. Point of Contact   6. Follow Through   7. Recovery

FOREHAND
TOPSPIN

Square Stance

KEYS:
Early Preparation
Balance
Timing

RECOMMENDED GRIPS:
Eastern, Semi-Western, Western forehand.[1]

1. **SPLIT STEP / REACT**
   - Get ready.[2]

2. **FOOTWORK**
   - Get to the ball early.[2]

Explosive first step.

3. **GOOD EARLY PREPARATION**
   A. Shoulder Turn
   - Turn the shoulders facing sideways (some players turn the shoulders leading with the elbow, and some even lift it, as the racquet is taken back. That's OK but not necessary).
   - Hips turn as well.
   - Chin should almost touch the *front* shoulder to ensure good trunk rotation.
   - Racquet end cap points forward, lining up with the incoming ball (and so the racquet head points back).[3]

- Arm relaxed.
- Wrist relaxed (loose grip).

Racquet goes back well before the ball bounces (as the ball crosses the net).

- Free hand stretches out in front (to maintain good balance).

B. Weight
- As a rule of thumb, your body weight should be where the racquet head is. In other words, when the racquet is taken *back*, your weight should be on your *back* foot. This is necessary because as the racquet goes forward to the point of contact, your weight (free energy) will transfer to the front foot, transferring all that energy into the shot (even in open stance shots).

C. Knees Bend
- As the racquet is taken back, your knees should be bent down as low as if you were sitting on a chair.

4. STOP AND STEP OUT IN FRONT
A. Stop and Step
- Stop to hit a controlled, balanced shot and step out in front, *toward* the target and not across, as in a closed stance. This effectively transfers the energy of your body links into the ball and toward the intended target.[4]

B. Sideways
- Body stays sideways while body motion stops, maintaining good balance.

C. Head Control
- The head should not move throughout the shot, especially at point of contact. The head is the center of balance of the body; by keeping it still, balance is maintained.

D. Eye Control
- Eyes should be locked on the ball. Watching the ball is an imperative tool for every player. This process starts by watching the opponent's racquet face at point of contact and continues by following the ball to your own bounce and point of

contact. Then, without losing track of the ball, continue to follow the ball back to your opponent's racquet. This sequence repeats until the point is over.
- At high-speed tennis, when the ball moves too fast, follow the ball with your eyes but focus especially when it gets to the *peak of the bounce* of your and your opponent's shot (the ball stops, before starts to come down). It is easier to visualize it this way.[5]

E. Forward Motion
- First, the knees extend up, starting the kinetic body chain (power production). Then the hips rotate forward, transferring the ground forces into the trunk; subsequently, the shoulders and arm rotate, then the elbow. Lastly, the wrist snaps forward, delivering the final force into the ball (note that elbow extension and wrist flexion occurs after point of contact). This kinetic chain of body links is one smooth, sequenced motion.[6]
- Make sure that the racquet head is lower than the ball before point of contact in order to generate topspin and good clearance over the net.
- Palm and racquet should face down for better topspin production.

- Free hand stretches out in front for balance.
- Relax arm and forearm (looser grip) so maximum acceleration can be attained.
- When more control is required, *stay low*, maintaining good balance (low center of gravity), to produce a solid point of contact (but no ground force production).

5. POINT OF CONTACT
- Eyes locked on the ball.

Racquet face looks at the target.

WITH PERFECT BASIC STROKES

- Racquet is square (face perpendicular to ground and racquet horizontal) and just out in front of the front knee at waist level (comfort zone).
- Elbow close to trunk, controlling the arm swing.
- Shoulders rotate forward, facing the net.
- Wrist firm (firm grip).
- Weight fully transfers to the front foot. Front knee extends. Back foot is on tiptoe, helping to maintain good balance.
- Racquet head achieves maximum acceleration at this point. By no means should the racquet slow down.

6. **FOLLOW THROUGH**
    - Eyes are steady at point of contact (striking zone) for a split second after the ball has left the strings (do not follow the ball with your eyes immediately after the point of contact). This will help to control accuracy of the shot, as well as helping to maintain balance.
    - The path of the racquet right after the point of contact is forward toward the target, keeping the face straight, and creating a feel of a longer contact with the ball (like hitting 3 balls continuously, or hitting through the ball), ensuring perfect aim.

PLAY WINNING TENNIS

- Wrist should be loose to help the racquet create more power (acceleration) and topspin (wrist snap).
- Racquet swings smoothly across the body, finishing high over the shoulder with the knuckles close to the ear (the end cap of the racquet should point forward to the intended target).
- Chin should be close to the right shoulder (ensures full shoulder rotation and good topspin).
- Free hand catches the racquet by the throat or just gets close to it.

A long smooth follow through ensures maximum acceleration at point of contact, and also relaxes the arm and shoulder.

7. RECOVERY

- With the forward momentum of the follow through, the back foot steps outside towards the sideline, pushing the body to shuffle to the "Recovery Site," or cross stepping to run to the next shot. Open stance players have the advantage of having their outside foot ready to push back to the "Recovery Site," saving one step.[2]

FOREHAND VARIATIONS

HIGH FOREHAND

Even though you always should hit the ball at your striking comfort zone (waist level), there will be situations that will be require you to hit at shoulder level, like a high kicking shot or an approach shot.

Follow the basics for any regular forehand, but stress:
- Hitting *through* with topspin, finishing high and over the ball.
- Good use of leg extension (getting a lift off the ground from impulse force).
- Using the back foot for balance on open stances.[2]
- Using the front foot for balance if attacking forward (approach shots).[2]

Note: Most high shots can be hit *off the ground*. Making contact in the air will add more energy (power) to the shot generated from the leg drive (leg muscles) as well as hitting the shot early, all together, a much more offensive shot. Dynamic balance must be maintained throughout the stroke, otherwise, the accuracy will be diminished.

PLAY WINNING TENNIS

TOPSPIN HIGH FOREHAND *FRONT VIEW*
Open Stance

1. Split Step / React   2. Footwork / 3. Early Preparation

Off the ground.

4. Point of Contact   5. Follow Through

Maintaining dynamic balance.

6. Recovery

FOREHAND SLICE

The Way Out

The slice forehand is not used as often as the slice backhand, but it is an option. Usually with a forehand, even on late point of contact and hit off the back foot, it is still possible to impart some topspin due to the position of the palm and the shoulder, producing a higher percentage shot (compared to the slice shot).

However, there are a few occasions where the slice forehand is a necessity. The obvious one is the *drop shot*. Another not so common instance is when reaching for the unreachable shot. Sometimes slicing those far wide shots (mostly on clay courts) is the only way to put one more ball over the net and maybe surprise your opponent by returning the impossible shot.

Slice for the approach shots can also be utilized, but most of the time you are better off hitting an aggressive topspin or flat approach shot, forcing your opponent to return a weak shot, giving you an easy time at the net.

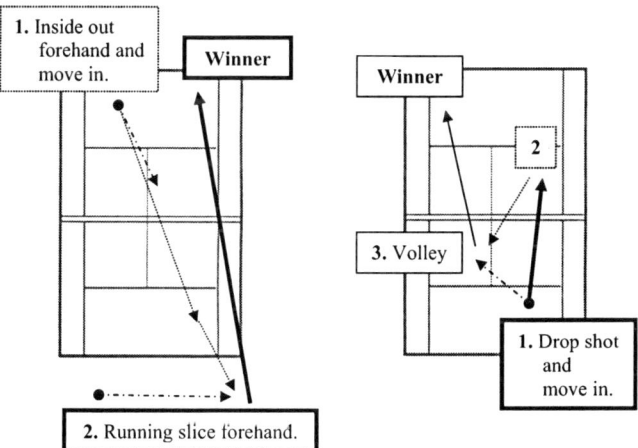

SLIDING SLICE FOREHAND *FRONT VIEW*

3. Early Preparation
(1. Split Step/React / 2. Footwork)

4. Point of Contact

5. Follow Through

SLICE FOREHAND *SIDE VIEW*

2. Footwork   3. Early Preparation
(1. Split Step / React)

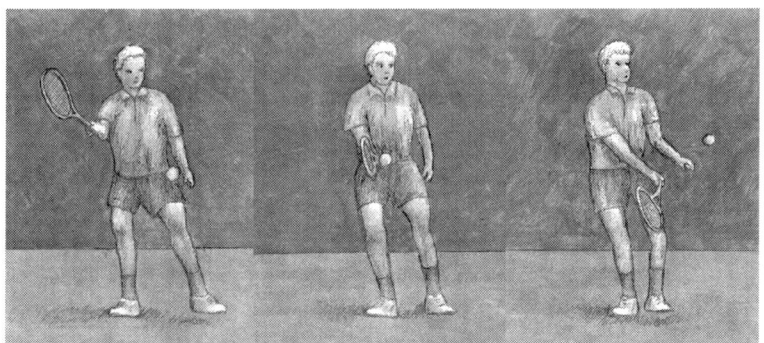

4. Point of Contact   5. Follow Through

6. Recovery

FOREHAND
SLICE

Open Stance

KEYS:
Balance
Timing

RECOMMENDED GRIP:
Continental[1]

1. **SPLIT STEP / REACT**
   - Get ready.[2]

2. **FOOTWORK**
   - Explosive first step.
   - Get to the ball early (drop shots).[2]
   - Get to the ball at full stretch (open stance will help you to reach and disguise those extreme far shots).[2]

3. **EARLY PREPARATION**
   A. **Shoulder Turn**
      - Turn the shoulders facing sideways.
      - Racquet goes back higher than normal. On defensive running wide shots, the racquet goes just slightly back.
      - Loose wrist.
   B. **Weight**
      - Weight on back foot in an open stance.[4]
   C. **Head Control**
      - The head should stay steady throughout the shot to maintain dynamic balance.
   D. **Eye Control**
      - Eyes should be locked on the ball.[5]
   E. **Forward Momentum**
      - Racquet swings down and through in a semi-circular motion as you stretch to reach the ball. Make sure that the racquet head is above the incoming ball before point of contact in order to generate underspin.[6] At full stretch, hips and shoulders face forward. Because this shot is an emergency shot, the body kinetic chain is not so effective, and, therefore, ground forces are not maximized.

4. POINT OF CONTACT
- Eyes locked on the ball.
- Racquet face slightly open.
- Ball can be hit at any height (shoulder, waist, or knee level).
- Arm and trunk at full extension (running stretch shot).

- Shoulders facing forward.
- Wrist firm. When underspin is used for a drop shot, loosen up the wrist (loose grip) to absorb the energy of the ball.

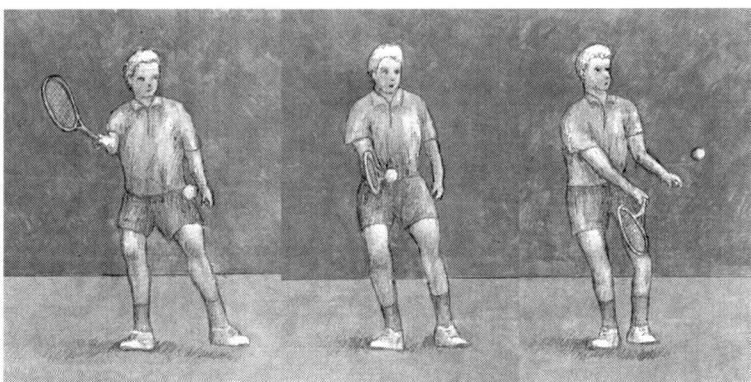

5. FOLLOW THROUGH
- Eyes steady at point of contact (striking zone) for a split second after the ball has left the strings (do not follow the ball with your eyes immediately after point of contact). This will help to control accuracy of the shot, as well as maintain balance.
- Racquet keeps dropping smoothly under the ball and *forward* toward the target, brushing the backside of the ball.[7]
- Palm and racquet open, facing upward, creating depth.
- No weight transfer is possible on wide shots due to the extreme stretch.

Eyes steady at striking zone.

- Wrist snaps forward (loose wrist) to compensate the lack of weight transfer.
- Free hand helps to control body balance.

6. RECOVERY
- The outside foot pushes the body to shuffle to the "Recovery Site" (or cross step to run to the next shot).[2]

---

[1] See book 1, chapter **"Grips"**
[2] See book 1, chapter **"Anticipation & Footwork"**
[3] See book 1, chapter **"Backswing Styles"**
[4] See book 1, chapter **"Stances"**
[5] See *Focus on the Ball* in book 4, chapter **"While Playing the Match"**
[6] See *Kinetic Body Chain* in book 1, chapter **"Stances"**
[7] See book 1, chapter **"Spins"**

BACKHAND

BACKHAND
ONE-HANDED

The "Set Up" Shot

In the last few years, the backhand, like the forehand, has become another weapon shot (topspin backhand). Even though this stroke is one of the most natural motions (the arm and racquet move away from the body), many players choose to develop this stroke as a tool to set up an aggressive attack by opening up the court. For example, a deep crosscourt backhand can leave your opponent on the defensive.

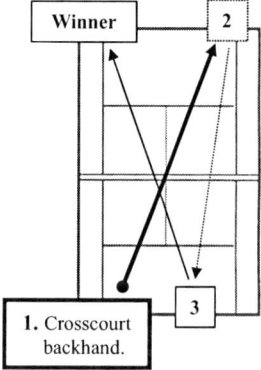

Footwork is the most important ingredient in a precise backhand, especially for the two-handed shot. The most important reason for that is that the shoulder that holds the racquet is out in front, which leaves the player no choice but to hit out in front of the front knee or to hit a weak shot. In contrast, the forehand can be hit a little bit late or behind and still be an aggressive shot (the shoulder that holds the racquet is behind). Therefore, quick footwork and early preparation for good timing are key factors for having an effective and consistent backhand.

PLAY WINNING TENNIS

ONE-HANDED TOPSPIN BACKHAND *FRONT VIEW*

1. Split Step / React   2. Footwork

3. Early Preparation   4. Stop and Step   5. Point of Contact

6. Follow Through   7. Recovery

WITH PERFECT BASIC STROKES

ONE-HANDED TOPSPIN BACKHAND *SIDE VIEW*

1. Split Step / React   2. Footwork

3. Early Preparation   4. Stop and Step   5. Point of Contact

6. Follow Through   7. Recovery

BACKHAND
TWO-HANDED

The Powerful "Set Up" Shot

The two-handed backhand has become the most popular shot at the professional level, especially among women. It is easy to grip and, for that reason, most beginner players choose this stroke (the lack of strength on the dominant arm is also a factor).

Loaded with powerful advantages, this shot can intimidate your opponent and force him into making an error.

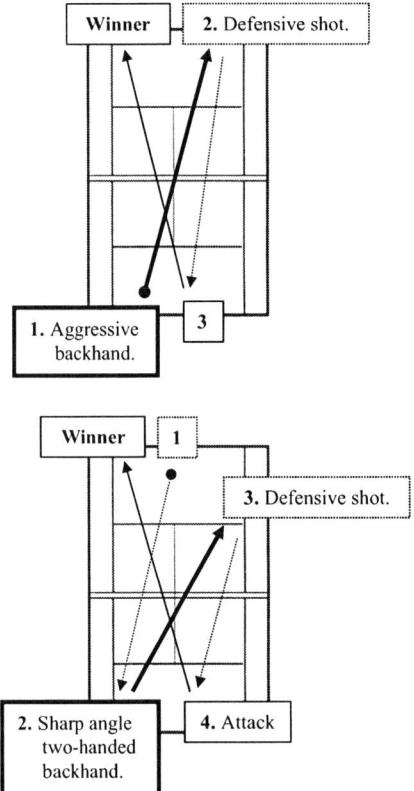

TWO-HANDED TOPSPIN BACKHAND *FRONT VIEW*

1. Split Step/React / 2. Footwork   3. Early Preparation

4. Stop and Step   5. Point of Contact

6. Follow Through   7. Recovery

PLAY WINNING TENNIS

TWO-HANDED TOPSPIN BACKHAND *SIDE VIEW*

1. Split Step / React   2. Footwork   / 3. Early Preparation

4. Stop and Step   5. Point of Contact

6. Follow Through   7. Recovery

BACKHAND
TOPSPIN

Square Stance

KEYS:
Footwork
Balance
Timing

RECOMMENDED GRIPS:
One-handed backhand: Eastern, Semi-Western backhand.[1]
Two-handed backhand: (bottom/top hand) Continental/Eastern forehand, Continental/Semi-Western forehand, Eastern backhand/Eastern forehand, Eastern backhand/Semi-Western forehand.[1]

1. **SPLIT STEP / REACT**
   - Get ready.[2]

2. **FOOTWORK**
   - Explosive first step.
   - Get to the ball early.[2]

3. **GOOD EARLY PREPARATION**
   A. **Shoulder Turn**
      - Hips turn as well.
      - Chin should almost touch the front shoulder to ensure good trunk rotation.
      - Racquet end cap points forward, lining up with the incoming ball (racquet head points back or just a little more for extra power on one-handed backhands).[3]

Racquet is back well before the ball bounce (as the ball crosses the net).

PLAY WINNING TENNIS

- Arm relaxed.
- Wrist relaxed (loose grip).
- Free hand holds racquet from the throat and helps to take the racquet back (one-handed backhand).

B. Weight
- As a rule of thumb, your body weight should be where the racquet head is. In other words, when the racquet is taken *back*, your weight should be on your *back* foot. This is necessary because as the racquet goes forward to the point of contact, your weight (free energy) will transfer to the front foot, transferring all that energy into the shot (even from open stances).

C. Knees Bend
- As racquet is taken back, so is your weight. Knees should be bent down as though you were sitting on a chair.

4. **STOP AND STEP OUT IN FRONT**

    A. Stop and Step
    - Stop to hit a controlled, balanced shot and step out in front toward the target, trying not to step across the body, as in a closed stance.[4] This effectively transfers the energy of your body links into the ball and toward the intended target.

    B. Sideways
    - Body stays sideways while body motion stops, maintaining good balance.

    C. Head Control
    - The head should not move throughout the shot, especially at the point of contact. The head is the center of balance of the body. By keeping it still, you maintain balance.

    D. Eye Control
    - Eyes should be locked on the ball. Watching the ball is an essential tool for every good player. This process starts by watching the opponent's racquet face and point of contact and continues by following the ball to your own bounce and point of contact. Then, without losing track of the ball, continue to follow the ball back to your opponent's racquet. This sequence repeats until the point is over.
    - At high-speed tennis, when the ball moves too fast, follow the ball with your eyes, but focus especially when it gets to the *peak of the bounce* of your and your opponent's shot (when the ball stops before it starts to come down). It is easier to visualize it this way.[5]

    E. Forward Motion
    - First, the knees extend up, starting the kinetic body chain (power production). Then the hips rotate forward, transferring the ground forces into the trunk. Unlike the two-handed backhand and the forehand, the hips and shoulders in the one-handed backhand do not rotate as much. Subsequently, the shoulders and arm rotate, then the elbow extends, and finally, the wrist snaps forward

(minimally on one-handed backhands), delivering the final force into the ball. This kinetic chain of body links is one smooth, sequenced motion. On the two-handed shot, the sequence of body links does not change, but the hips and shoulder (upper body) rotate forward (facing the net) as the follow through is completed.[6]
- Make sure that the racquet head is lower than the ball before the point of contact in order to generate topspin and get good clearance over the net.
- Relax arm and forearm (looser grip) so maximum acceleration can be attained.
- When more control is required, stay *low*, maintaining good balance (low center of gravity) to produce a solid point of contact (but no ground force production).

5. POINT OF CONTACT
- Eyes locked on the ball.
- Racquet square (face perpendicular to ground and racquet horizontal) and just out in front of the front knee at waist level (comfort zone).

Shoulders and hips rotate forward.

Shoulders and hips stay sideways.

Racquet face looks at the target.

- Dominant arm straight but not locked, elbow in and not leading forward.
- During the *one-handed* shot, the shoulders and hips stay sideways, lining up with the target until the completion of the stroke. On the *two-handed* backhand, the shoulders and hips rotate forward as the racquet completes the follow through.
- Wrist firm.
- Racquet head achieves maximum acceleration at this point. By no means should the racquet slow down.
- Weight fully transfers to front foot. Front knee is extended. Back foot is on tiptoe to help maintain good balance.

PLAY WINNING TENNIS

6. FOLLOW THROUGH

- Eyes steady at point of contact (striking zone) for a split second after the ball has left the strings (do not follow the ball with your eyes immediately after point of contact). This will help to control accuracy of the shot, as well as maintain balance.
- The path of the racquet right after the point of contact is forward toward the target, keeping the face straight, and creating a feel of a longer contact with the ball (like hitting 3 balls continuously or hitting through the ball), ensuring perfect aiming.

- Racquet swings smoothly forward toward the target and finishes high, with knuckles at shoulder level and racquet head pointing up (thumb up) on the one-handed shot. During the two-handed shot, the hands finish close by the right ear (racquet end cap looks forward to the target).
- Chin should stay close to the front shoulder.
- Wrist should be slightly looser by the end of the stroke in order to relax the arm, but wrist snap is minimal on the one-handed backhand.

Thumb up.

Free hand snaps back, controlling the balance and adding acceleration to the racket (one-handed backhand).

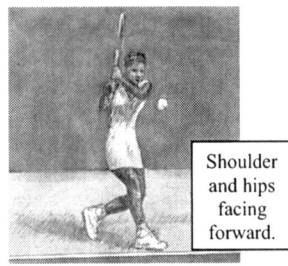

Shoulder and hips facing forward.

WITH PERFECT BASIC STROKES

7. RECOVERY
- With the forward momentum of the completed follow through, the back foot steps outside towards the sideline, pushing the body to shuffle to the "Recovery Site" or cross stepping to run to the next shot. Open stance players have the advantage of having the outside foot ready to push back to the "Recovery Site," saving one step.[2]

Note: Many players refer to the one-handed backhand as a harder stroke to master, even though swinging away from the body is a more natural motion than the forehand motion. The difference lies in the position of the dominant shoulder (the right shoulder for right-handed players) for each stroke. When the dominant shoulder is in front, like in a one-hand backhand shot, the timing that starts from the racquet back to the completion with the follow through becomes more of an issue (point of contact must be out in front of the body). Likewise, on the forehand stroke, the dominant shoulder is back at the preparation stage, making the shot easier to handle (more time to prepare for the point of contact).

ONE-HAND VS. TWO-HAND

One-Hand Advantages:
(Two-Hand Disadvantages)

- **Better reach**
  The one-handed backhand has far more reach than the two-handed shot. If the two-handed backhand is held with the Continental grip on the bottom hand, the one-handed slice can be utilized, and therefore, there is no reach disadvantage.
- **Ease of footwork**
  A two-handed backhand requires getting closer to the ball than the one-handed shot.
- **Quicker "into the body" return of serve**
  Two-handed players can get jammed more easily.
- **Easy to slice**
  Natural downward swing.
- **Easy to volley**
  Forearm muscles are better prepared for the backhand volley.
- **Ease of high/low shots**
  The one-handed shot has a bigger window for making contact (mid-trunk to mid-thigh) than the restricted two-handed shot (that is why a two-handed player requires quicker and more precise footwork).

Two-Hand Advantages:
(One-Hand Disadvantages)

- **Powerful**
  The use of the second hand makes this stroke an extremely powerful weapon. With the one-handed shot, only the fingertips are behind the grip, requiring a strong forearm to produce a firm shot.
- **Deceiving**
  The two-handed shot is hard to read, and it is easier (than the one-handed shot) to change direction of the ball.
- **Greater Shock Absorption** due to the two hands holding the grip.
- **Sharp Angle Shots**
  Due to the combination of wrist action and firmness, sharper angles can be hit more easily.

WITH PERFECT BASIC STROKES

BACKHAND VARIATIONS

HIGH BACKHAND

Even though you always should hit the ball at your striking comfort zone (waist level), you will have situations, like a high kicking shot or an approach shot, that will be require you to hit at shoulder level.

Follow the basics for any regular backhand
1. **Split Step / React**
2. **Footwork**
3. **Early Preparation**
4. **Point of Contact.** Not always possible to stop and step, but stress:
   - Hit well out in front and off the front foot especially when attacking forward.
   - Good use of leg extension (getting a lift off the ground from impulse force).
   - Hit *through* with topspin, finishing high and over the ball.
5. **Follow Through**
6. **Recovery**

Note: Most high shots can be hit *off the ground*. Making contact in the air will add more energy (power) to the shot generated from the leg drive (leg muscles) as well as hitting the shot early; all together, a much more offensive shot. Dynamic balance must be maintained throughout the stroke; otherwise, your accuracy will be diminished.

PLAY WINNING TENNIS

TOPSPIN HIGH BACKHAND *FRONT VIEW*

2. Footwork **3. Early Preparation**
(1. Split Step / React)

4. Point of Contact   **5. Follow Through**   **6. Recovery**

Off the ground.

Maintaining dynamic balance.

BACKHAND SLICE

The Great Defense

The slice backhand might not be a powerful shot like the topspin backhand, but it still can be as effective as any other ground stroke when applied at the right time. The slice can keep your opponent off balance by changing pace (floaters as well as aggressive slices) and spin (low bounces). It is just another weapon for your arsenal.

There are other situations where underspin can come in handy. By imparting underspin on an "approach shot," the ball will float deep, buying you time to reach the net, and because of the low bounce, your opponent will be forced to hit up, setting up an easy volley for you. Also, an extreme amount of underspin must be imparted on a drop shot (with a loose wrist) for the ball to bounce low and short and, consequently, to make it unreachable.

Even though the shoulder that holds the racquet is out in front, the slice backhand lets you hit a bit behind the normal topspin shot point of contact (due to the continental grip), thus becoming an excellent defensive shot.[4] Still, footwork and early preparation is essential for this one-handed slice shot.

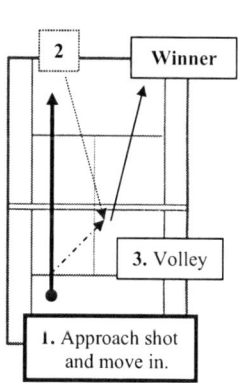
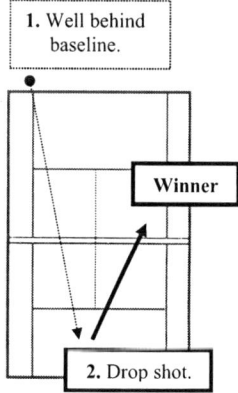

ONE-HANDED SLICE BACKHAND *FRONT VIEW*

3. Early Preparation   4. Stop and Step
(1. Split Step/React   /   2. Footwork)

5. Point of Contact

6. Follow Through

ONE-HANDED SLICE BACKHAND *SIDE VIEW*

4. Stop and Step   5. Point of Contact
(1. Split Step/React / 2. Footwork / 3. Early Preparation)

6. Follow Through

TWO-HANDED SLICE BACKHAND *FRONT VIEW*

4. Stop and Step **5. Point of contact**
(1. Split Step/React / 2. Footwork / 3. Early Preparation)

6. Follow Through

WITH PERFECT BASIC STROKES

TWO-HANDED SLICE BACKHAND *SIDE VIEW*

4. Stop and Step   **5. Point of Contact**
(1. Split Step/React / 2. Footwork / 3. Early Preparation)

6. Follow Through

BACKHAND SLICE

Square Stance

KEYS:
Balance
Timing

RECOMMENDED GRIPS:
One-handed backhand: Continental[1]
Two-handed backhand: (bottom/top hand) Continental/Eastern forehand, Continental/Semi-Western forehand.[1]

1. **SPLIT STEP / REACT**
   - Get ready.

2. **FOOTWORK**
   - Explosive first step.
   - Get to the ball early.[2]

3. **GOOD EARLY PREPARATION**
   A. Shoulder Turn
   - Hips turn as well.
   - Chin should almost touch the front shoulder to ensure good trunk rotation.

   - Racquet back. Face slightly open and high (above the shoulder).
   - Keep arm and wrist relaxed (Continental grip for one-handed shot).
   - Free hand holds racquet at the throat and helps to take the racquet back (one-handed backhand).

WITH PERFECT BASIC STROKES

    B. **Weight**
- Weight on back foot (transferred forward as the racquet travels to the point of contact).

    C. **Knees Bend**
- Knees slightly bent.

4. **STOP AND STEP OUT IN FRONT**
   A. **Stop and Step**
   - Stop to hit a controlled, balanced shot and step out in front toward the target.
   - For a defensive slice shot, when pulled wide, have a closer stance.[4]

   B. **Sideways**
   - Body stays sideways while body motion stops, maintaining good balance.

   C. **Head Control**
   - The head should stay steady throughout the shot.

   D. **Eye Control**
   - Eyes should be locked on the ball.

   E. **Forward Motion**
   - Driving the racquet end cap into the ball (**1**), swing the racquet head down (**2**) and through in a semi-circular motion as your weight transfers *forward* into the ball. Make sure that the racquet head is above the incoming ball before the point of contact in order to generate underspin.
   - Hold the racquet with a looser grip to relax the arm and forearm, therefore attaining maximum acceleration.

Hips and shoulders rotate forward.

   - Shoulders and hips stay sideways, lining up to the intended target (one-handed backhand).

PLAY WINNING TENNIS

- Because power is not the main ingredient of the slice backhand, the leg extension (first link of the kinetic body chain) happens only at the end of the stroke as the follow through is performed. Hips and shoulders have very little rotation (one-handed backhand), leaving only gravity (racquet weight), forward momentum (created by the body weight as you hit through), and some leg drive to create power. This forward motion is one smooth, sequenced swing. On the two-handed slice, the hips and shoulders rotate forward, facing the net by completion of the follow through.
- Due to the two hands holding the grip (two-handed backhand), low shots are much more difficult to reach and execute than when using the one-handed slice.

5. POINT OF CONTACT

- Eyes locked on the ball.
- Racquet face slightly open, out in front. The angle of the racquet face depends on the depth and height of the shot needed. For a floater shot the racquet face should be much more open than for an aggressive slice shot (practically perpendicular with the ground at impact).

WITH PERFECT BASIC STROKES

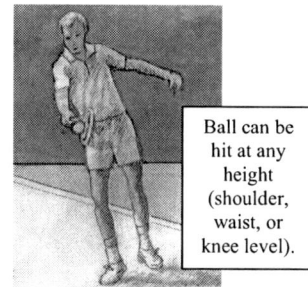

Ball can be hit at any height (shoulder, waist, or knee level).

- Chin should almost touch the front shoulder.
- Arm straight, elbow in (but not locked) and close to trunk.
- Shoulders sideways lining up to the target (one-handed backhand).
- Wrist firm. When underspin is used for a drop shot, or for a slower shot, the wrist should be loose (absorbs energy).
- Weight fully transfers to the front foot. Front knee extends. Back foot is on tiptoe to help maintain good balance.
- Racquet head achieves maximum acceleration at this point. By no means should the racquet slow down.

6. FOLLOW THROUGH

Hips and shoulder facing forward.

- Eyes steady at point of contact (striking zone) for a split second after the ball has left the strings (do not follow the ball with your eyes immediately after point of contact). This will help you control accuracy of the shot, as well as maintain balance.

PLAY WINNING TENNIS

- Racquet keeps dropping smoothly downward and forward toward the target, brushing the backside of the ball; finish high at shoulder level, with racquet face completely open, controlling depth and height.

- Wrist should be loose to help the racquet create more power and underspin.
- Free hand stays behind, controlling the balance (one-handed backhand).

7. RECOVERY
- Follow the ball if an approach shot is hit or recover to the "Recovery Site" if you stayed on the baseline.[2]

---

[1] See book 1, chapter **"Grips"**
[2] See book 1, chapter **"Anticipation & Footwork"**
[3] See book 1, chapter **"Backswing Styles"**
[4] See book 1, chapter **"Stances"**
[5] See *Focus on the Ball* in book 4, chapter **"While Playing the Match"**
[6] See *Kinetic Body Chain* in book 1, chapter **"Stances"**

VOLLEY

VOLLEY

The Winning Advantage

To have a winning game, you'll need to be able to come up to the net and finish the point. The volley is a simple mechanical shot. Most of it is just watching the ball (with a quick reaction) and good footwork.

Strategically, coming up to the net will raise your chances of winning a point, because when you hit a quick simple shot (volley) close to the net, you cut off the reaction and execution time of your baseline opponent, who must hit a more complex and time-consuming shot (ground stroke). Also, at the net, you have the possibility of opening up the court with a much more pronounced angle.

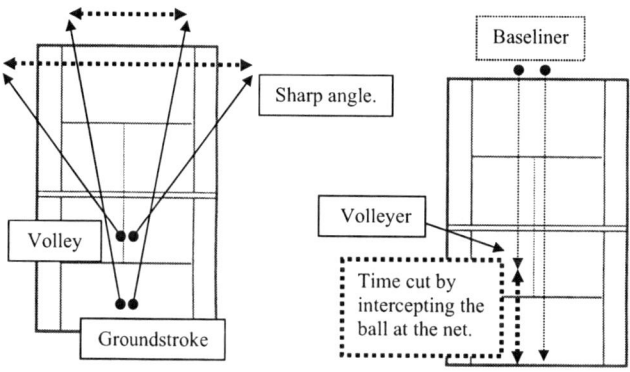

PLAY BETTER TENNIS

FOREHAND VOLLEY *FRONT VIEW*

1. Split Step / React   2. Footwork   3. Step / 4. Point of Contact

5. Follow Through   6. Recovery

FOREHAND PUNCH VOLLEY *SIDE VIEW*

1. Split Step / React / 2. Footwork / 3. Step

4. Point of Contact   5. Follow Through

6. Recovery

ONE-HANDED BACKHAND PUNCH VOLLEY *FRONT VIEW*

1. Split Step / React   2. Footwork

3. Step   4. Point of Contact   5. Follow Through

WITH PERFECT BASIC STROKES

ONE-HANDED BACKHAND PUNCH VOLLEY *SIDE VIEW*

1. Split Step / React

2. Footwork   3. Step / 4. Point of Contact / 5. Follow Through

PLAY BETTER TENNIS

PUNCH VOLLEY

Forehand and One-Handed Backhand

KEYS:
Eye on the ball (early & quick reaction)
Footwork
Timing
Simplicity (no backswing, no follow through)

RECOMMENDED GRIPS:
Continental. Eastern forehand and Eastern backhand for beginners.[1]

1. SPLIT STEP / REACT
- Get ready.[2]
- Immediate reaction (to forehand or backhand).
- Racquet and elbows out in front of the body. A common mistake is to split with the elbows tucked to the body, thereby slowing down the volley reaction.

Feet on toes (ready to split).

Ready to react (after the split).

2. FOOTWORK
- First thing, right after the split, is to *set up the racquet*, ready to hit the ball (early and quick reaction), by loading the weight on the outside foot.
- Cover the shot quickly, moving forward toward the ball, cutting off the angle,[2] with the racquet ready (on the side, facing flat to the ball) to punch (for the backhand volley bend the elbow slightly to facilitate the stroke) and hit aggressively.

WITH PERFECT BASIC STROKES

Set up the racquet.

Loading the outside foot.

Moving with the racquet ready.

- The free hand helps to control the balance (out in front on the forehand and holds the racquet from the throat on the backhand) as you get to the ball.
- Wrist relaxed.

3. STEP TOWARD THE BALL
- Before contact, step forward toward the ball (medium and low height shots). Step with foot opposite your racquet hand for the forehand volley (left foot) and the same foot as the hand that holds the racquet for the backhand volley (right foot).
- This step will help your shoulder to turn a little sideways, placing your body in a better biomechanical position (mechanically sound shot).
    - A. Allows your racquet to go back enough to have a controlled punch (racquet should not go farther back than your back shoulder).
    - B. Sets your body in a comfortable position to see the ball well (from the side, not across the strings).
    - C. Helps to attack the ball forward (weight transfers forward, creating momentum) and to hit it through without stopping.
- The elbows should be close to the side of the body and slightly out in front to ensure a consistent point of contact.
- On high volleys, you may need to step forward right after contacting the ball, especially when moving forward fast. This way you will be able to control the shot better without pulling down the racquet.

PLAY BETTER TENNIS

On high volleys, step forward *after* point of contact.

On low volleys, step *before* contact.

- When volleying far from the net (close to the service line) and a *deep shot* is required (first volleys),[2] a slightly longer back swing (further back than your back shoulder) is going to be necessary; just be aware that the longer the backswing, the harder to control the point of contact (too much power).

4. **POINT OF CONTACT**
   - Eyes locked on the ball.
   - Without completely stopping, punch through the ball.
   - The shoulder should be slightly sideways and the point of contact should be aligned with the front shoulder (or just in front) for a more aggressive volley.
   - Racquet arm should be straight but not locked (at the elbow).
   - Racquet head should be higher than the wrist, forming a "V" between the racquet and the forearm. This "V" will provide stability, control, and power. That is why it is important to maintain this "V" in all situations, especially on low shots.
   - On low volleys, keeping the "V" up will keep the racquet face straight, and help the ball to clear the net low. When you are at the net, the last thing you want is to volley up, leaving your opponent with an easy put-away shot. Try to keep the "V" by getting low with a wide step forward, and bending down from your knees (back knee will be almost touching the ground).
   - On high volleys, drive the racquet end cap into the ball first, and then the racquet head should impact the ball.

WITH PERFECT BASIC STROKES

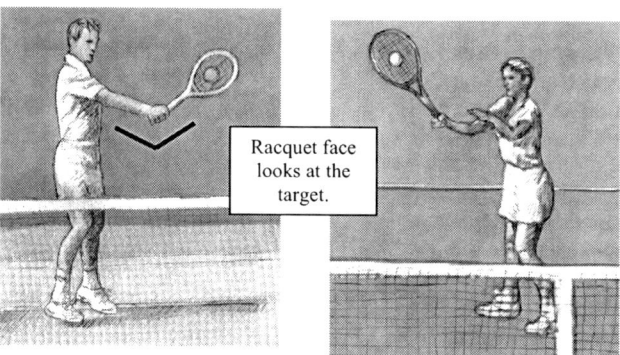

Keeping Up the "V"

Note: When punching the ball, make sure not to swing the racquet. The punch happens by stepping forward towards the ball and keeping the arm firm (firm wrist), making a consistent point of contact.

- A small amount of underspin or slice should be imparted to the ball. The spin will help control the flight of the ball, and it will also add a low bounce, forcing your opponent to hit the ball up, which will give you an easy put-away second volley. Be careful not to scoop the ball to impart spin. Instead, think of punching the ball through with the racquet face straight (on edge), and then slightly open the racquet face as the ball leaves your strings (not a downward swing).

Note: Make sure not to slap at the ball (wrist action). This will create an inconsistent, weak, angular shot.

PLAY BETTER TENNIS

- Free hand stays out in front for the forehand and back for the backhand, controlling the body motion and balance.
- Unless you need to absorb energy for a touch shot like a drop shot or drop volley (loose wrist), keep your wrist firm for a crisp shot.

Remember: Don't look for *power* on volleys but for *control* (placement). Power will be generated using the energy (speed) of the incoming ball and your forward momentum (moving and stepping forward with a firm wrist).

5. FOLLOW THROUGH
- Eyes stay steady at point of contact (striking zone) for a split second after the ball has left the strings (do not follow the ball with your eyes immediately after point of contact). This will help you control the accuracy of your shot, as well as maintain balance.
- Wrist relaxed.
- Follow the ball with the strings just slightly forward and through the ball for a compact feel (bottom edge of racquet follows forward slightly, opening the racquet face). Make sure to do this slight angle change of the racquet face *immediately after* the point of contact (imparting underspin) and *not before* (that would create a floater volley which is too easy to return).

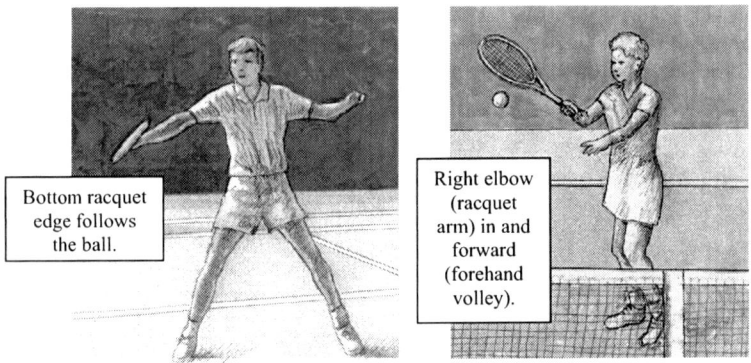

Bottom racquet edge follows the ball.

Right elbow (racquet arm) in and forward (forehand volley).

- Keep your head still throughout the stroke to maintain dynamic balance.

6. RECOVERY
- Racquet quickly recovers to the center of the body and above the net on low volleys to prepare for the next shot.
- The back foot steps outside toward the sideline, pushing the body to shuffle to the "Recovery Site."[2]

WITH PERFECT BASIC STROKES

Racquet recovers to the center of the body.

Back foot steps outside towards the sideline.

VOLLEY VARIATIONS

"RIGHT AT YOUR BODY" VOLLEY

Most often this shot must to be played as a one-hand block backhand volley. Using the racquet as a shield, you can defend your body and win the point with this quick reaction shot.

The forehand block volley will only be used when the ball is coming straight at your right armpit (right-handed players). If the ball comes right at your body but not at a high speed (no pace), step away from the ball and treat it as a regular forehand volley, trying to step forward if possible. When the ball comes right at you with a lot of pace, it becomes a very difficult shot to control and the only way to effectively volley it is by dodging the ball with the shoulders (right shoulder pivots backward, trying to avoid the ball). At the same time the racquet takes its place (where right shoulder was), making a solid blocking volley (point of contact will be slightly behind but aligned with your head).

Remember: However you choose to take this "right at your body" volley (as a forehand or as a backhand), make sure there is no hesitation, only a quick reaction.

PLAY BETTER TENNIS

BLOCK VOLLEY

Quick Switch from forehand to backhand and vice versa.

KEYS:
Split Step Reaction
Simplicity (just a block)

RECOMMENDED GRIP:
Continental[1]

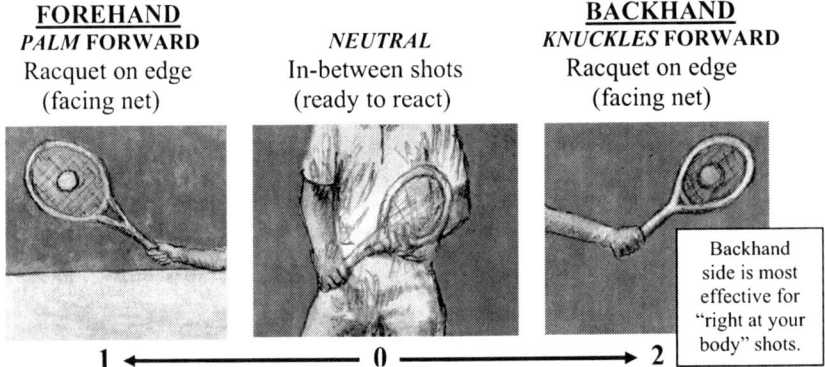

FOREHAND	*NEUTRAL*	**BACKHAND**
PALM **FORWARD**	In-between shots	*KNUCKLES* **FORWARD**
Racquet on edge	(ready to react)	Racquet on edge
(facing net)		(facing net)

1 ←——————— 0 ———————→ 2

Backhand side is most effective for "right at your body" shots.

A. **SPLIT STEP / REACT**
   Racquet in the center of your body, ready to react, at neutral position (**0**).

B. **QUICK READY**
   Work with your palm forward (**1**) for the forehand or knuckles forward (**2**) for the backhand to develop a quick reaction as you load the outside foot.

WITH PERFECT BASIC STROKES

TWO-HANDED BACKHAND VOLLEY

Though there is nothing wrong volleying with two hands, especially if you've just started to play the game, the one-handed volley has many more advantages than the two-handed shot.

Two-hands on the grip will shorten your reach, jam you on shots "right at your body," slow you down on quick exchanges, and will make your "serve and volley" game completely unsuccessful (extremely difficult on low volleys). On the other hand, it is a comfortable, powerful shot (waist and high shots). However, power is not an issue on volleys.

Remember, if you have a two-handed backhand ground stroke, the two-handed backhand volley will come naturally. Developing the one-handed shot will not be easy (dominant hand forearm muscles might need conditioning). Start by preparing the shot with two hands **(1, 2)**, and then as you make contact with the ball **(3)** release the top hand **(4)**. Once the forearm muscles get stronger, you will be able to control the stroke better.

Note: The recommended grips for the two-handed backhand volley with the top hand release **(4)** are any combination that holds the bottom hand with "Continental" grip.[1] This grip will allow you to control the shot by imparting some slice without compromising power. If the top hand is not released, play with the same grip used for the two-handed backhand stroke.

PLAY BETTER TENNIS

LOB VOLLEY

The lob volley is a combination of the lob and the volley used as a variation of the regular punch or drop volley. Even though it is considered a volley because the ball is hit in the air without the bounce, this shot is more of a control-touch shot than an offensive put-away volley. The ball is contacted with an open-faced racquet and a firm wrist in order to pinpoint the lob.

It is mostly used when your opponent is running forward to get a drop shot or low volley and is especially effective on clay, when changing direction is most difficult.

DROP VOLLEY

The drop volley is a shot that, when played at the right time, has the power to confuse your opponent, disrupt his rhythm, and finish the point easily (usually your opponent expects a forceful offensive volley, not a ball that just clears the net). However, make sure your opponent is behind the baseline (some players are extremely fast), and keep up the element of surprise (don't overuse it).

Also, notice that the most effective surface for a drop volley is on slow courts, like clay or Har-Tru, because the ball, which carries heavy underspin and no power, will bounce very low on the slow surface, making a tough shot to reach, practically unreachable.

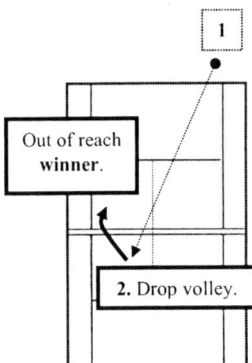

64

WITH PERFECT BASIC STROKES

FOREHAND DROP VOLLEY *FRONT VIEW*

1. Split Step / React   2. Footwork

3. Step / 4. Point of Contact   5. Absorb Shock

FOREHAND DROP VOLLEY *SIDE VIEW*

1. Split Step / React

2. Footwork / 3. Step   4. Point of Contact   5. Absorb Shock

WITH PERFECT BASIC STROKES

ONE-HANDED BACKHAND DROP VOLLEY *FRONT VIEW*

1. Split Step/React   2. Footwork

3. Step / 4. Point of Contact 5. Absorb Shock

ONE-HANDED BACKHAND DROP VOLLEY *SIDE VIEW*

3. Step   4. Contact   5. Absorb Shock
(1. Split Step/React / 2. Footwork)

DROP VOLLEY

Forehand and One-Handed Backhand

KEYS:
Timing
Loose Wrist

RECOMMENDED GRIP:
Continental[1]

- Same procedure as a punch volley, but before making contact with the ball, loosen up the grip to have a relaxed wrist and absorb most of the energy of the ball.

Loose wrist.

- There is no follow through with this shot. The racquet dies right after the point of contact, insuring no transfer of energy into the ball.

STAB VOLLEY

Forehand and One-Handed Backhand

A stab volley is an emergency shot that, in most cases, will result in a drop volley. The difference is that a stab volley is a reaction shot; it is not premeditated. Footwork is not effective because the ball is too far away; therefore, a lunge is necessary.[2] The racquet should be kept straight (on edge) throughout the point of contact, and the wrist loosens up right after, producing a stabbing motion (underspin), and a drop volley.

Move first with the outside foot as you push off with the other foot.

1. Lunge   **2. Point of Contact (Stab)**

Free hand controls the body balance.

3. Absorb Shock

---

[1] See book 1, chapter **"Grips"**
[2] See book 1, chapter **"Anticipation & Footwork"**
[3] See book 4, chapter **"Volley Strategy"**

SERVE

WITH PERFECT BASIC STROKES

SERVE

The Killer Strength

The serve can be the greatest weapon, but it also is a double-edged sword. If your service is effective (powerful, good placement, spin variety), it can open up the point aggressively and, therefore, make it easy to control and win the point. On the other hand, if your serve is poorly executed, your opponent will take charge of the point, no matter how aggressive your strokes are.

Psychologically, the serve can be a great confidence builder, or buster. When your serve is on, your game and strategy will fall into place, but when your serve is off, you can lose all of your confidence in your strokes and game plan.

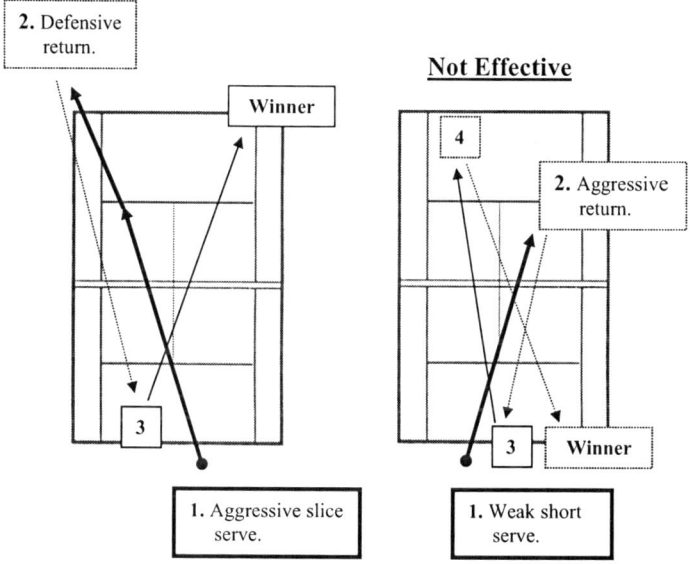

PLAY BETTER TENNIS

FIRST SERVE *FRONT VIEW*

1. Stance   2. Begin Swing

3. Upward Motion

4. Point of Contact   5. Follow Through

WITH PERFECT BASIC STROKES

FIRST SERVE *SIDE VIEW*

1. Stance   2. Begin Swing

3. Upward Motion

4. Point of Contact   5. Follow Through

PLAY BETTER TENNIS

FIRST SERVE

KEYS:
Rhythm & Timing
Loose & Relaxed (Smooth Swing)
Balance
Controlled Toss
Simplicity

RECOMMENDED GRIPS:
Continental. Eastern backhand, Eastern forehand (beginners).[1]

1. STANCE
- Stand comfortably (loose & relaxed), about one foot from the center mark, with fairly straight posture.
- Knees slightly bent.
- Feet shoulder width apart. Front foot is about an inch behind the baseline at a 45-degree angle to it. The back foot is parallel to the baseline. Toes (both feet) should be lined up towards the intended target.
- Face sideways. Sideways shoulder and hips ensure a good body rotation, which will generate angular momentum.
- Hands together, racquet pointing to the aimed service box.
- Weight starts on the front foot.
- Wrist relaxed.

WITH PERFECT BASIC STROKES

2. **BEGIN SWING**
   - Start routine (always the same way).
   - Hands start together.
   - Racquet is out in front and the weight is on the front foot.
   - Hands drop down together and start a *slow, smooth,* upward motion with the racquet arm slightly delayed (**B**). Some players manage to lift both arms up at the same time, which is all right as long as you can keep good smooth rhythm (but it slows down racquet head acceleration).
   - The weight shifts from the front foot (**A**) quickly to the back foot (**B**) and then back to the front foot (**C**) in a rocking motion.

A   B   C

   - Holding the ball by the fingertips, very gently and slowly lift the hand slightly forward, aiming to the right net post (45-degree angle with the baseline).[2] The ball should be tossed with the arm straight (lift from the shoulder), in a straight upward motion, without bending the elbow or wrist, avoiding any kind of spin on the ball. Release the ball above eye level (**B**) to ensure a straight up toss. This arm stays up for a split second after the release, then comes down to the chest (at point of contact). The ball should be placed as high as the height of the tip of the racquet stretched up, this way the ball drops a couple of inches to the center of the racquet (point of contact) without picking up any speed from the vertical fall (gravity).
   - How to take the racquet back (backswing serve) is a matter of style. Some have it long and some have it compact, but all backswings should be smooth, rhythmically correct, and should get to the same position (**C**).
   - Left hip (front hip) shifts forward (**C**).
   - Elbow up (90 degrees between the elbow and trunk).

PLAY BETTER TENNIS

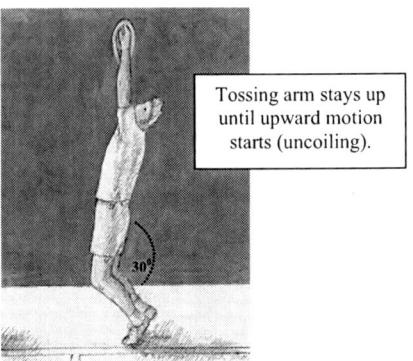

Tossing arm stays up until upward motion starts (uncoiling).

- At this point, the knees bend down, about 30 degrees, and shoulders should be fully rotated, about 140 degrees with the baseline (coil), for maximum power (acceleration) production.

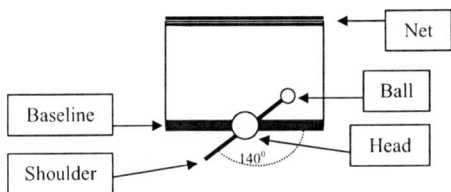

COILING
(Top View)
- Weight and hip shift forward.
- Shoulder rotation.
- Elbow up.
- Tossing arm up.

WITH PERFECT BASIC STROKES

- As the ball gets to the point of contact area, the racquet drops behind the back. The elbow stays up 90 degrees or more from the trunk, pointing back.

3. UPWARD MOTION
- First, the knees straighten up, pushing off the front foot and starting the kinetic chain of energy production. This exploding, upward force will impel the body off the ground.
- Then, as the hips and shoulders rotate forward, the body weight is added to the ground forces (body moves forward to the tossed ball) generated by the kinetic chain.
- Elbow points up and moves forward with the shoulder rotation. The racquet is still behind the back but away from it (no back scratch), getting ready for maximum acceleration. Note that the palm of the hand that holds the racquet always stays facing down (knuckles up), canceling any extra forward wrist movement, and increasing the spin and *pronation* (note that the racquet *edge* is facing up).

Racquet away of body.

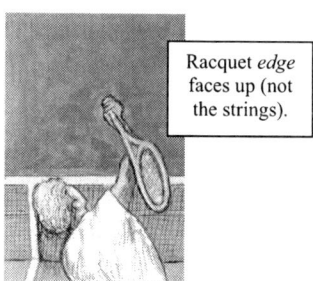

Racquet *edge* faces up (not the strings).

- Arm and wrist extend up as racquet accelerates and applies *spin* to the ball at point of contact.[3]

PLAY BETTER TENNIS

4. POINT OF CONTACT

- Shoulder and hip are completely rotated, facing the net.
- Palm and racquet turn inward for full pronation.

Racquet *edge* turns inward, making the strings face the target and stroking the ball.

- Make contact when the ball reaches the peak of the toss or just starts to come down (the ball carries no speed at the peak or very little as it starts to come down).
- Hit up and forward (all the energy is concentrated to the point of contact, not to the service box).
- Racquet, arm, trunk, and front foot are almost in straight line.
- Thumb of hand that holds the racquet points up.
- Wrist firm.
- Racquet face looks at target for perfect aiming. At this point racquet head reaches maximum acceleration.

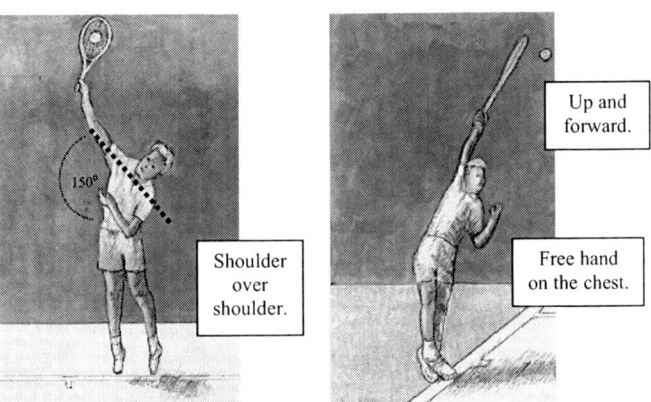

Shoulder over shoulder.

Up and forward.

Free hand on the chest.

- Shoulder is almost in a vertical position (150 degrees or more between the arm and trunk), and the right shoulder reaching as high as possible (the higher the reach, the greater the margin for net clearance).
- Tossing arm moves into the chest, so racquet arm snaps (accelerates).

WITH PERFECT BASIC STROKES

5. **FOLLOW THROUGH**
   - Right after contact, the racquet continues forward as *chin stays up* (this prevents the ball from dropping into the net).

Inner racquet edge turns inward (pronates) as the strings follow the ball.

   - Wrist snaps (looser wrist), adding speed to the ball (last link of kinetic chain). Thumb points down and elbow up.

Thumb points down as the wrist snaps and the elbow turns up.

Chin stays up.

   - First, land on front foot inside the court, then the back foot comes along. Let forward momentum carry you forward.[4]

81

PLAY BETTER TENNIS

- Right shoulder completely rotates forward.
- Racquet finishes on the left side of the body (flush with the leg).

6. RECOVERY
- Continue moving forward for serve and volley game.[5]
- Make several splits steps, backing up quickly for baseline game.

FOR MORE POWER

- Make sure your weight is fully transferred forward (fall inside the court after point of contact).
- Focus on acceleration, not on strength, don't muscle the shot.
- Make sure motion is smooth and continuous. Do not stop when racquet is behind the back.
- Rotate shoulders well (150-degree angle with the baseline) and keep racquet away from the back when coiling (shoulder rotation).
- Use kinetic body chain as the source of power (ground forces + body links = acceleration).
- Focus on acceleration towards the point of contact, not the service box.
- As with any other stroke, you can manipulate equipment to adapt to your game style. To gain more power, lower the string tension (trampoline effect) and/or add lead tape to the head of the racquet, around the 9 and 3 o'clock spots. Also, you may consider switching to a stiffer (but heavier) racquet, maybe even a longer-bodied racquet (longer than the traditional 27" long) with an oversize head.

SERVE VARIATIONS
SPINS AND SECOND SERVES

Good servers not only have the ability to place the serve effectively, they can also keep their opponent guessing by changing pace and spin. Mixing up the service is a must for an advanced player.

Many players believe that a second serve is like a first one but slower. If you follow that thought, your serve will look more like a weak push than an aggressive delivery. Most of the ingredients of the first serve make up the second serve. However, some adjustments (grips, ball toss placement, focus of acceleration-spins, etc.) are needed (as discussed in Chapter 1, "Spins").

Focus of Acceleration-Spins
The major difference between a topspin first serve and a topspin second serve is the focus of acceleration. The direction of the energy is the same, but for a first serve, the forward vector (hollow arrow) is the focus of acceleration. In other words, the racquet should accelerate faster at that point and in that direction. For a second serve, the focus of acceleration is the brushing behind the ball vector (black arrow), and therefore, more spin than power will be created, producing a higher percentage second serve.

Energy Vectors
Racquet face should follow the direction of the vector (gray arrow), extending upward with the body and arm, and brushing the backside of the ball *7 to 1* (black arrow) with the wrist. After contact, the wrist snaps and racquet follows straight forward (hollow arrow) to the target.

Remember: Do not slow down your 2nd serve; instead replace *power by spin*.

---

[1] See book 1, chapter **"Grips"**
[2] See *Placement of the Toss* in book 1, chapter **"Spins"**
[3] See *Applying Spin on the Serve* in book 1, chapter **"Spins"**
[4] See *Serve Footwork Patterns* in book 1, chapter **"Anticipation & Footwork"**
[5] See chapter **"Serve and Volley"**

RETURN OF SERVE

RETURN OF SERVE

The Silent Weapon

The return of serve should be treated as more than just another shot. A good "returner" can steal the momentum from a server and make him pay for a weak second serve. Generally speaking, it is important for any player to develop a good return, but it's essential for a player who doesn't own a big serve: by breaking the server, the returner can be more relaxed when it's time for him to serve. Two of the best all time returners, Andre Agassi and Jimmy Connors, both relied on the return of serve to keep the pressure on the server and finally break his game (note that they were not known for killer serves).

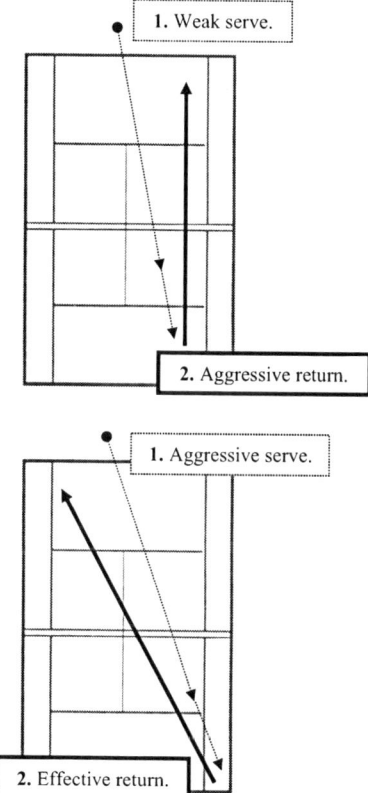

PLAY BETTER TENNIS

FOREHAND RETURN *FRONT VIEW*

1. Ready Position / Split Step / React   2. Shoulder Turn

3. Step   4. Point of Contact

5. Follow Through   6. Recovery

WITH PERFECT BASIC STROKES

FOREHAND RETURN *SIDE VIEW*

1. Ready Position / Split Step / React

2. Shoulder Turn   3. Step   4. Point of Contact

5. Follow Through   6. Recovery

PLAY BETTER TENNIS

ONE-HANDED BACKHAND RETURN *FRONT VIEW*

1. Ready / Split Step / React   2. Shoulder Turn

3. Step   4. Point of Contact

5. Follow Through   6. Recovery

WITH PERFECT BASIC STROKES

ONE-HANDED BACKHAND RETURN *SIDE VIEW*

1. Ready Position / Split Step / React   2. Shoulder Turn

3. Step   4. Point of Contact

5. Follow Through   6. Recovery

PLAY BETTER TENNIS

TWO-HANDED BACKHAND RETURN *FRONT VIEW*

1. Ready Position / Split Step / React

2. Shoulder Turn / 3. Step / 4. Point of Contact

5. Follow Through   6. Recovery

WITH PERFECT BASIC STROKES

TWO-HANDED BACKHAND RETURN *SIDE VIEW*

1. Ready Position / Split Step / React 2. Shoulder Turn

3. Step   4. Point of Contact   5. Follow Through

6. Recovery

RETURN OF SERVE
FLAT OR TOPSPIN

Forehand and Backhand

KEYS:
Quick Early Reaction
Aggressiveness
Firm Blocking Wrist (Compact Backswing)

RECOMMENDED GRIPS:
Same grips used for topspin forehand and backhand groundstrokes.[1]

1. READY POSITION[2] / SPLIT STEP / REACT
- Stand in a spot where you can cover the forehand as well as the backhand return, usually a foot or two away from the intersection of the baseline and the singles sideline. Waiting position can vary depending on the depth, speed, and spin of the opponent's serve, but for the first serve, it is commonly about one to two feet behind the baseline, and for the second serve, a foot inside the baseline. As rule of thumb, if you need more time to react, back up as much as necessary in order to place the ball back in play. If the serve is slow, move up as much as you can in order to hit the ball on the rise and attack.[3]
- Racquet out in front, preferably in the center of your body (neutral position).
- Wrist relaxed.
- Free hand (fingertips) holds the racquet at its throat.
- Knees bend for low center of balance, and upper body leans slightly forward from the waist (for quick reaction).
- Eyes fix on opponent's toss and point of contact.

WITH PERFECT BASIC STROKES

- **Footwork:**
  A. Traditional

  - Feet comfortably apart, about shoulder width and parallel to the baseline.
  - Split step forward with both feet just before opponent hits the ball.[4]
  - Quickly react for a forehand or a backhand.

B. One Foot Out

  - One foot is out in front. It doesn't matter which one is out as long as it's always the same one (get into a routine).
  - Step forward with the back foot before the opponent hits the ball and split step forward.[4]
  - Quickly react for a forehand or a backhand.

PLAY BETTER TENNIS

2. SHOULDER TURN
- Load the outside foot by rotating the shoulders and hips accordingly.

Free hand out in front.

Free hand helps on the backswing.

- Racquet goes back with a *compact backswing* for a quicker reaction.[5] Focus is on quick shoulder turn rather than racquet back. Shoulder turn will guarantee enough power without compromising control. How far the racquet should go back depends on the serve. As a rule of thumb, the faster the serve, the more compact the backswing should be. For some very fast serves, use a block type return.

WITH PERFECT BASIC STROKES

3. STEP
- Step forward to get some momentum behind the ball and generate pace.
- On very fast serves when a quick reaction is the only way to return, hit the ball in open stance.²

4. POINT OF CONTACT

- Eyes locked on the ball.
- Knees extend, hips and shoulder rotate forward (forehand and two-handed backhand), and with a firm, tight grip, block the ball. On the one-handed backhand, hips and shoulders stay sideways, lining up with the target area.
- Racquet face aims at the target area.
- Free hand snaps backward as racquet makes contact with the ball, helping to maintain control and balance (one-handed backhand).

PLAY BETTER TENNIS

5. FOLLOW THROUGH
- Racquet face follows forward toward the target.
- Racquet finishes over the shoulder, imparting some topspin. On faster serves, it is better to use a block return, finishing with the racquet firm out in front (like a volley).
- Dynamic balance throughout the stroke must be maintained. Keeping the swing compact and simple will allow you to gain accuracy and consistency, regardless of the speed of the serve, and it will also help you recover quickly for the next shot.

- Free hand remains back throughout the follow through (one-handed backhand).

Head steady throughout the follow through.

6. RECOVERY
- Immediately with the forward momentum of the follow through, the back foot steps outside, pushing back to the "Recovery Site" or follow your return forward attacking the net.[4]

WITH PERFECT BASIC STROKES

RETURN VARIATIONS

CHIP RETURN

The chip return is a great weapon for returning fast, powerful serves and for use against "Serve & Volley" players. Mostly used on the backhand side (one-handed slice[6]), this shot will keep the ball low (slicing effect) forcing a "Serve & Volley" player to volley up, and it will prevent a baseliner from attacking as easily as he would, with a high bouncing return. Most importantly, this return gives you more time to charge the net, because the floating effect of the underspin takes longer to reach the opponent's side. Therefore, you can reach a more aggressive position closer to the net.

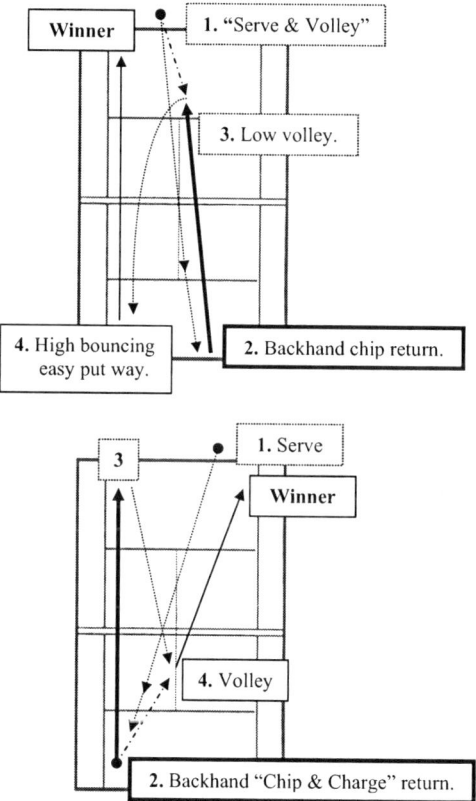

99

PLAY BETTER TENNIS

CHIP RETURN OF SERVE *SIDE VIEW*

1. Ready Position   Split Step

React   2. Shoulder Turn

3. Step / 4. Contact   5. Follow Through

CHIP RETURN OF SERVE

One-Handed Backhand and Forehand

KEYS:
Quick and Early Reaction
High Preparation
Firm Blocking Wrist
Balance

RECOMMENDED GRIP:
Continental[1]

1. READY POSITION[2] / SPLIT STEP / REACT
- Quickly react to the opponent's serve as the ball leaves the strings, loading the outside foot.

2. SHOULDER TURN
- Same as a regular return, but racquet is prepared above shoulder level.

3. STEP
- Step forward to get some momentum behind the ball and generate pace and spin.

4. POINT OF CONTACT
- Eyes locked on the ball.
- Meet the ball well out in front.
- Knees extend as the ball is punched like a volley.
- Arm straight.
- Wrist firm.
- Impart a bit of slice by slightly opening the racquet face.

PLAY BETTER TENNIS

- Shoulders are sideways.
- Free hand stays back, maintaining balance.

5. FOLLOW THROUGH
- Racquet face and arm continues forward toward target.
- Racquet face opens as ball leaves the racquet, right after the point of contact.
- Weight completely transfers to front foot.

Head steady throughout the follow through.

6. RECOVERY
- Recover to the "Recovery Site"[4] or charge the net.

---

[1] See book 1, chapter **"Grips"**
[2] See book 1, chapter **"Stances"**
[3] See book 4, chapter **"Return of Serve Strategy"**
[4] See book 1, chapter **"Anticipation & Footwork"**
[5] See book 1, chapter **"Backswing Styles"**
[6] See chapter **"Slice Backhand"**

OVERHEAD

OVERHEAD SMASH

The Shot of No Return

Today, winning tennis just from the baseline is almost impossible, but attacking the net is risky if you do not own an effective and powerful overhead.

The motion of the overhead is similar to the serve. However, there are a number of differences that a player must know in order to own a consistent overhead. One important point is that the overhead ball is derived from an opponent's *lob*, consequently, the smasher must get into a position to hit it (on the serve, the ball is in control, in server's hand). Also, consider that the higher that ball is, the more downward acceleration (gravity) will affect the ball. Therefore, good timing is critical, which is why the backswing of an overhead should be abbreviated.

The overhead, like the serve, is a confidence booster. When consistent, well placed, and with a good amount of power, it can definitely be called "the shot of no return."

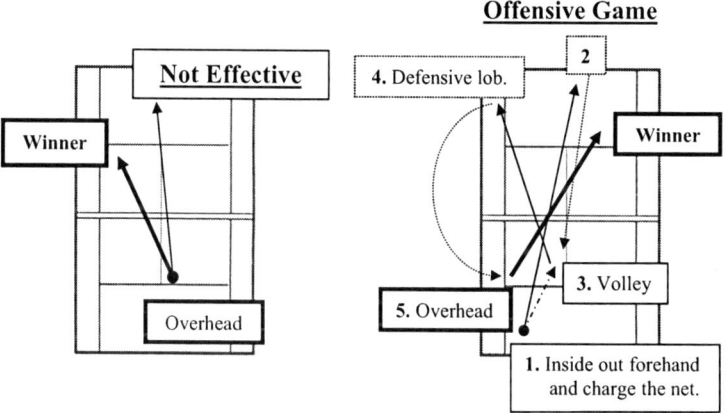

PLAY BETTER TENNIS

OVERHEAD SMASH *SIDE VIEW*

2. Recognizing a Lob   3. Footwork
(1. Split Step / React)

4. Coiling / 5. Upward Motion / 6. Point of Contact

7. Follow Through

WITH PERFECT BASIC STROKES

OVERHEAD

KEYS:
Early Preparation
Quick Footwork
Good Timing

RECOMMENDED GRIP:
Continental, Eastern forehand (beginners).[1]

1. **SPLIT STEP / REACT**
   - Get ready.[2]

2. **RECOGNIZING A LOB**
   - Quickly recognize and react to opponent's lob.

- Step back with the right foot (this action allows the shoulders and hips to get sideways, getting ready for easy and quick movement[2] in order to get under the ball). As you step back, the racquet goes back in an abbreviated backswing and the free hand extends up. Fingertips point to the ball, as if trying to catch the ball. This will help you get under the ball more quickly and precisely.

107

PLAY BETTER TENNIS

3. FOOTWORK
- Good footwork is essential for an effective overhead. Proper footwork is needed to get the body into position. As the ball reaches its height, quickly move back and get under it as if it was going to fall on top of your head or chest, or place yourself under the ball as if it was a ball toss on a serve.[2]

4. COILING
- Racquet goes behind and away from the back.
- Elbow is high, pointing up.
- Shoulders and hips are sideways.
- Knees bend (not low).
- Weight is off the back foot.

Keep the back fairly straight to hit a flat overhead.

WITH PERFECT BASIC STROKES

5. UPWARD MOTION
- Knees extend. If you need to jump, keep dynamic balance.[2]
- Free hand is out in front.

6. POINT OF CONTACT
- Eyes locked on the ball.
- Shoulder and hips rotate forward, facing the net.
- Weight shifts forward. If a jump is necessary, keep dynamic balance.
- Racquet, arm, and body fully extend (right shoulder stretches upward).
- Point of contact happens in front and slightly to the right.
- Palm and racquet pronate.[3]
- Free hand goes to the chest (this stops the shoulder, producing a whipping effect).
- For aiming, use the palm holding the racquet. Wherever the palm faces, the racquet face will direct the ball.
- If close to the net (around the service line), clearance of the net is not an issue, so hit the overhead *flat*.
- Chin up.

Back straight.

7. FOLLOW THROUGH
- Wrist snaps, adding speed to the ball (last link of kinetic chain).
- Racquet continues forward as pronation continues.
- Chin stays up.
- Wrist relaxes and arm follows to the left side of the body (flush with the leg).
- Back foot steps forward.

PLAY BETTER TENNIS

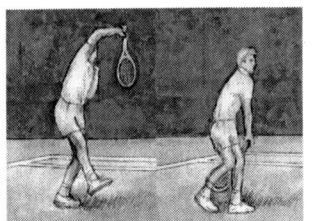

Thumb down and elbow up.

Front View   *Side View*

8. RECOVERY
- Split step and get ready for a surprise return.

OVERHEAD VARIATION

BACKHAND SMASH

- Difficult shot (requires strong shoulder and back muscles).
- Use only when a regular overhead is not an option (opponent's lob is well into your backhand side).
- Use continental or eastern backhand grip.

1. After the split step, react and move under the ball.
2. Turn sideways into a backhand position (racquet is back, elbow is up and pointing to the ball).
3. With the weight transferred onto the back foot, push off and snap into the high ball.
4. Contact the ball as high as possible and slightly in front of the body. The free hand snaps back, producing a whipping effect.
5. Right after the point of contact, the arm and racquet follow the ball (as much as possible), finishing with the back practically facing the net.

---

[1] See book 1, chapter **"Grips"**
[2] See book 1, chapter **"Anticipation & Footwork"**
[3] See *Palm Pronation* in chapter **"Serve"**

Printed in the United States
120091LV00001B/121/P